Change Leadership Intelligence (CLQ)
A Definition

By

GEORGE W. RIDEOUT, D.B.A.

Dedication

For those who detest change and hunger for an edge...

Contents

Foreword

I presented a roughly drawn abstract of the following research paper at a conference in late 2011. After my presentation, I remember the audience feedback was simply, "Wow…you have a lot of work on your hands. This can take years to develop." I thought to myself, "That is encouraging. At least everyone did not think I was crazy for proposing a new intelligence." I left the conference with a renewed sense of vigor and dedicated myself to developing the abstract into a research paper with meat. Since the conference, the abstract has spawned a detailed literature review encompassing theory and suppositions from a rich range of sources. I admittedly have enjoyed every minute of this journey, although it has just begun.

My general interest in change leadership studies began during my career working in the U.S. metal building industry. I often internally questioned decisions and ideas regarding initiatives, especially after seeing many go up in smoke immediately or have only limited staying power. My disappointment after seeing so much of my peers' hard work and financial loss caused me to question why these initiatives failed. Thus I began my quest to find out why change fails so often. Soon after this, I decided to advance my education. I went back to graduate school and finished my MBA, a long overdue project that had been an on-again, off-again love affair for years. This time, education piqued my interest, and I decided to pursue a doctoral degree. I am not sure if it was my age (maturity) or the innate desire to learn, but I yearned for more education.

My doctoral studies provided a rich education in leadership theory. This lead to my capstone project or dissertation focused on change leadership in, what else, the U.S. metal building industry! I had the wonderful opportunity to work with and learn from a Delphi panel of seasoned industry executives who gave their valuable time to share insight into how they identify, manage, and use change in their organizations. The research data revealed a change leadership model that may benefit any industry. The model also provides support for the research paper in this book.

This research paper represents the first step in establishing a new idea: proposing a conceptual definition. There is much to learn about the idea of change leadership intelligence, and this research paper merely scratches the surface. Much has been written about change leadership, but drawing the link to intelligence is a new twist on a popular and important topic. There is work to prove CLQ's existence and answer the many what-ifs. The more I look at the world, the more I see the traits discussed in this paper in leaders today. Are these leaders *change* leaders? Do they exhibit *change leadership intelligence*? You be the judge. Read the paper. What do you think?

---*George W. Rideout*

Change Leadership Intelligence (CLQ)
A Definition

In the three short decades between now and the twenty-first century, millions of ordinary, psychologically normal people will face an abrupt collision with the future. Citizens of the world's richest and most technologically advanced nations, many of them, will find it increasingly painful to keep up with the incessant demand for change that characterizes our time. For them, the future will have arrived too soon.

---Toffler (1970)

x

1 Research Paper

Drucker (1999) identified change leadership as a critical skill-set for the twenty-first century organization. This mandate requires a new form of leadership, in which leaders become stimulants for driving organizational innovation (Bennis & Goldsmith, 1997). Change forces, such as a global economy and rapid technological advances, create an environment in which leaders can no longer rely on trusted traditions of doing business to maintain a competitive advantage. Instead, leaders must not only guide their organizations to become flexible, agile entities that can change or assimilate to meet market demands but also learn to create strategies that spawn change (Hamel & Prahalad, 1994). Tuominen (2000) offered a similar argument when he linked learning to continuous improvement and sustainable competitive advantage, in which leaders develop organizational skills to meet constantly changing strategic demands in the business environment. These arguments create a call for the learning organization.

An integral part of this equation is the learning process evident in the organization, and how leaders may develop change leadership in themselves and their people. Research suggests various intelligences play a significant role in how people in organizations learn. Because change leadership represents an important construct in developing core competencies, and sustainable competitive advantage, it becomes obvious that change leadership may be a unique set of skills or intelligence. The literature is rich with data on intelligences, but a gap exists when investigating change leadership and its link to intelligence. This gap creates an opportunity to explore the notion, viability, and existence of change leadership as a form of intelligence.

The purpose of this paper is to explore the concept of change leadership as a unique intelligence and to posit a model and working definition. A review of the literature revealed that systems theory and various intelligences, including cultural, emotional, logical-mathematical, practical, and social, provide support for change leadership intelligence (CLQ). The inductive or deductive reasoning process and the concept of change leadership in the literature lend further support. The paper also offers guidelines for an assessment tool to measure CLQ that strengthens the scholarly significance for the leadership field, and future research opportunities.

Literature Review

Change pervades life, personally and professionally. Technology is the foremost agent for change, creating boundary-less organizations (McLean, 2007). The days of slow methodical change are gone, forcing leaders to reconsider strategy and become forward thinking (Mann, 2010).

Drucker (1999) stated that assumptions form reality. This statement points to the need for leaders to question, expand, enhance, and change their thinking. Leaders must become cognizant of change in their environment and the systems precipitating change. More important, they must become open to identifying mechanisms to manage and use change to promote a competitive advantage or leadership position. Rideout (2012) offered a definition for change management that aligns with this concept:

> Change management is a dynamically structured team process of planning and execution in which leaders

recognize change and adapt the organization to meet altered

conditions in the business environment, created by forces

such as competition, product innovation, and scarcity of

resources (p. 105).

Keywords in the definition, such as *recognize*, *adapt*, and *altered*,

suggest dependence and interaction with leader intelligence. Ulrich

(1996) believed expertise would become a defining factor for future

leaders, making title less important. This results-oriented argument

supports the need for twenty-first century leaders to develop their

knowledge base, including intellectual capacity, and various

intelligences. The argument also creates a new reality for the

twenty-first century organization, in which employee's company-

wide effect leadership, previously reserved for the c-suite.

Change leaders exist in all parts of life. To grasp the idea of

change leadership intelligence and posit a definition, identifying the

interrelationship of known intelligences to change leadership

intelligence may be helpful. Change leadership intelligence (CLQ)

is likely a combination of skills representing an array of

intelligences, working asynchronously and synchronously

depending on the situation. Intelligences such as practical

(common-sense), emotional (intra-personal) and social (inter-personal), logical-mathematical, and cultural each may play a critical role in formulating a CLQ quotient. Further exploring these intelligences also may help demonstrate the importance of developing CLQ and the uniqueness of the intelligence.

CLQ may be linked to how individuals think when presented with a problem. Exploring inductive versus deductive reasoning may provide answers. Another opportunity exists in studying the traits and behavior of change leaders in society, past and present. This study may point to characteristics evident in change leaders. Finally, reviewing existing change models from the literature may help formulate a definition of CLQ.

Intelligence

Intelligence studies became popular in the 20th century. Work by Albrecht (2006, 2007), Fiedler (1981), Gardner (1983, 1999), Goleman (1995, 1998), Salovey and Mayer (1990), and Sternberg, Kaufman, and Grigorenko (2008) shaped the intelligence studies field. Scanning the literature reveals burning questions creating controversy and precipitating future study: what intelligence(s) compose the ideal leader psyche, and does a specific intelligence stand out?

Academics, business leaders, and researchers offer diverse arguments for specific intelligences. Goleman (1995, 1998) and Albrecht (2006, 2007) made compelling cases for emotional, practical, and social intelligences, with each being the most relevant to effective leadership. Gardner (1983) and Sternberg, Kaufman, and Grigorenko (2008) saw intelligence as a mixture of skills coming from multiple areas in the human psyche. The Gardner (1983) posits opened the door to unique intelligence studies, spawning arguments for intelligences such as emotional, practical, and social.

Fiedler (1981) saw controversy when linking intelligence to leadership; he offered a unique perspective to intelligence and leadership studies. According to Fiedler, research shows little evidence that intelligence determines a leader's effectiveness, and studies comparing a leader's experience and effectiveness shows less correlation. Instead, Fiedler posited that skills and situation working in tandem determine leadership success; finding the best leader for a job requires understanding the situation. Charan (2009) in the context of the global economic meltdown evident in the early

6

2000s stated "only by synchronizing people as a companywide team can you obtain focus, speed, urgency, and flexibility, making and executing decisions faster" (p. 18). Fiedler and Charan confirm leadership should no longer be a c-suite activity, but a company-wide initiative in which all employees become leaders.

The consistent theme among the schools of thought is that developing leadership requires awareness and the willingness to learn and choose a new way of thinking. Obviously, leadership for the modern twenty-first century organization is a motley combination of skills and resolve, in which people in the organization form a collective of leadership capability. Every person in the organization holds a critical role in the collective success, with all becoming stewards of information and knowledge, and identifying and using change to create a leadership position for the organization. In this context, the role of systems and the change leader is evident.

Practical Intelligence

Practical intelligence (PI) describes gut instinct or common sense (Sternberg et al., 2000; Albrecht, 2007). Street smart is another common phrase used to identify a person with high PI (Peters,

1987). Formally, Albrecht (2007) defined PI as "the mental ability to cope with the challenges and opportunities of life" (p. 41). This definition suggests a link between PI and other intelligences such as emotional and social in which people must manage their inner and external self.

Peters (1987) extended this definition to encompass the idea of street smarts versus book or school smarts. According to Peters, the difference is that book smarts represent a constant learned or solved by someone else, and conversely street smarts require adaptability to real-world issues. This adaptability includes problem identification and determining the best course of action. Gut instinct or intuition plays a significant role in the diagnosis of the real problem, and often these skills are not taught in academia, such as teaching students how to be creative. The complexity of teaching these concepts is often beyond the reach of the classroom (Peters, 1987). Fortunately, all is not lost. Albrecht (2007) argued that people could enhance their PI by learning thinking skills.

Emotional and Social Intelligence

Emotional and social intelligence represent closely related intelligences, intra-personal, and inter-personal respectively.

8

Emotional intelligence is "the ability to monitor one's own and others' feelings and emotions, to discriminate among them and to use this information to guide one's thinking and actions" (Salovey & Mayer, 1990, p. 189). Albrecht (2006) described social intelligence as "the ability to get along well with others and to get them to cooperate with you" (p. 3). Salovey and Mayer (1990) saw emotional intelligence as unique, but closely related to social intelligence. This argument suggests the interconnectedness of intelligences, and confirms earlier assertions by Gardner (1983, 1999) who posited the theory of multiple intelligences, in which he identified eight forms of intelligence, including: linguistic, logical-mathematical, musical, naturalistic, spatial, bodily-kinesthetic, interpersonal, and intrapersonal.

Emotional intelligence represents intra-personal skills covering five distinct areas: a) self-awareness, b) emotion management, c) self-motivation, d) empathy, and e) relationship management (Goleman, 1995). Meta-cognition or self-awareness may help people function at a higher level, and become conscious of their deep feelings that may not be obvious (Goleman, 1995). This self-awareness points to the depth of the human psyche, and confirms that humans may be able to choose or control moods, and sub-conscious behavior.

Social intelligence encompasses inter-personal skills, and how we as humans interact with other humans. According to Gardner (1983), a person with inter-personal skills will have "the ability to notice and make distinctions among other individuals and, in particular, among their moods, temperaments, motivations, and intentions" (p. 239). This description suggests a heightened awareness of the external environment in people with inter-personal skills.

Emotional intelligence may be critical to CLQ because it lends credence to an individual's ability to accept and deal with problems. This suggests people who are comfortable and confident with their inner selves will accept change more quickly than those who are not. Social intelligence broadens this link to the external environment suggesting that as an individual gains a heightened awareness of those around them, including changing behaviors, the individual may be able to identify change more quickly than others. Coupling emotional and social intelligence together indicates these intelligences are active ingredients in the CLQ mix.

Logical and Mathematical Intelligence

Gardner (1983) in his theory of multiple intelligences identified logical and mathematical intelligence as a component of the human psyche. Piaget and his work on human thought processes lay the groundwork for today's study of logical and mathematical intelligence. Bellanca, Chapman, and Swartz (1997) described logical and mathematical intelligence as "the ability to use inductive and deductive reasoning, solve abstract problems, and understand complex relationships of mathematical reasoning and the scientific process" (p. 105). The ability to identify important links between events, and potential outcomes makes logical and mathematical intelligence integral to developing change leadership intelligence.

Cultural Intelligence

Cultural intelligence became the new buzzword in the late twentieth century, spearheaded by rapid technological change, and the new global economy. Earley and Mosakowski (2004) described cultural intelligence as "an outsider's seemingly natural ability to interpret someone's unfamiliar and ambiguous gestures the way that person's compatriots would" (p. 140). An important construct in developing cultural intelligence is reducing ethnocentrism.

Ethnocentrism is the belief that one's own ethnic group is superior to others (Anonymous, 1996). Triandis (2006) argued that people could reduce ethnocentrism by working to understand different cultures, such as through exposure. On organizational level leaders may place employees in new environments to discourage ethnocentrism, and at an individual level exposing one's self to new environments such as by joining new groups may help. Reducing ethnocentrism and developing cultural intelligence requires an open-mind, and the willingness to accept the 'new'. Exposure to new environments and cultures suggests a willingness to set fears and inhibitions aside; an important construct in developing CLQ in which people must step outside their comfort zone, accept the unknown, and embrace change.

Systems Theory

Systems theory provides rationalization for the inter-relatedness of everything that happens in the world, and provides a foundation for understanding change leadership intelligence. Von Bertalanffy (1969) posited these relationships when he created

General Systems Theory (GST) during the height of World War II. Later work by Boulding (1956), Johnson, Kast, and Rosenzweig (1964), Mockler (1968), Laszlo (1996), and Senge (2006) have each shaped systems theory offering unique, but similar perspectives.

According to von Bertalanffy (1969), systems exist in three forms real, conceptual, and abstract. Real systems represent entities independent of the observer, such as humans, and animals, conceptual provide evidence of thought-based intelligences, and abstract systems are another form of conceptual systems creating a link between concept and reality (von Bertalanffy, 1969). Although, von Bertalanffy offered a distinction between real and conceptual systems, he recognized the gray area, or the complexity of systems thinking. This complexity shows the interrelationship or influence between systems.

Senge (2006) stated systems "are bound by invisible fabrics of interrelated actions, which often take years to fully play out their effects on each other" (p. 7). Humans are part of this fabric, making our individual ability to see the big picture sometimes difficult (Senge, 2006). According to Senge, this concept explains the human tendency to narrowly focus our attention, therefore, missing the real forces causing change, and ultimately leading to our inability to solve the real problem.

Inductive versus Deductive

How leaders make decisions may influence the outcome. An important, construct in the decision-making process is how the leader analyzes the decision. This includes how the leader creates a plan to make the decision reality. If a leader can envision the desired end-result or think deductively, logically the leader may be able to positively influence the decision-making process. If the leader, however, has limited capacity for creating an end-state vision, and thinks inductively, the leader may not be able to construct a plan to get the organization from point A to point B. Arora (2003) stated that most people think inductively, and have difficulty making the link between long-term vision, and current reality; deductive thinkers are visionary. This forest from the trees mentality may explain why some leaders are more successful than others, and lends support for developing critical thinking skills.

Facione (2011) argued that critical thinking skills include: "interpretation, analysis, evaluation, inference, explanation, and self-regulation" (p. 5). Deductive and inductive reasoning are facets

14

of critical thinking skills (Zori & Morrison, 2009), and align with the Facione inference argument. According to Facione, inference refers to drawing conclusions, and more important to deduce consequences.

Zori and Morrison (2009) believed critical thinking is a learned skill people may develop through doing. For instance, by reflecting in a journal, people may learn to critically analyze their thoughts, and inevitably draw linkages between ideas (Zori & Morrison, 2009). These linkages may support the ability to become a visionary or deductive thinker.

Philley (2005) used the scientific method to show the cognitive systematic structure of critical thinking and decision-making. The scientific method involves seven steps including:

1. Recognizing the problem;

2. Creating a problem definition;

3. Data collection;

4. Data analysis;

5. Constructing potential outcomes;

6. Testing the outcomes; and

7. Selecting the best scenario (Philley, 2005)

The scientific method provides a synergistic approach to critical thinking, and points to a skill-set suggesting the need for a system perspective when analyzing a problem or making a decision.

Change Leaders

Kanter (1983) believed human perception creates the impetus for change. This belief supports the notion that leaders who are knowledgeable about their environment may identify change more quickly than competitors who lack this knowledge. The argument also suggests organizations may gain an advantage if they can expand this knowledge base to include employees throughout the organization beyond the c-suite. Creating a company-wide learning environment in which all employees become change leaders may be part of this equation.

According to Drucker (1999), change leaders see opportunity in change and seek out change in the internal and external environment. Thus, they will a) create policies in the organization to support future change, b) design strategies to identify change in the environment, c) create strategies to implement change at the organizational and external level, and d) identify "policies to balance change and continuity" (Drucker, 1999, p. 73).

16

Landale (2004) expanded on the Drucker (1999) and Kanter (1983) perspective when he stated that effective change leadership is founded on self-awareness and developing intelligences needed to identify and manage change. Change leadership is a result of an individual's willingness to learn and become cognizant of his or her environment.

Hoffer (1952) described those experiencing change as "misfits," because they are removed from the norm and experience a new environment. The term *misfits* is a misnomer, however, as Hoffer explains using a new employee as an example. Hoffer reasoned the new employee is a misfit but exhibits a heightened sense of awareness and passion caused by the new workplace environment. The new employee will go beyond the call of duty to perform well. The crux of the argument is how leaders can create misfits in every organization to encourage this new employee passion in every employee. Perhaps the answer lies in creating a heightened sense of awareness and perceptions in every employee or, more important, developing change leadership intelligence (CLQ).

Change Leaders in Society

An effective way to understand such a complex subject as intelligence is to examine the traits and characteristics of those who exhibit the intelligence. Change leadership intelligence (CLQ) is unique because it not only requires the integration of practical, social, and emotional intelligence. It also requires an out-of-the-box mindset that coincides with transformational leadership. Transformational leaders are visionaries who inspire others to achieve a new purpose, a fundamental characteristic of those with above average CLQ.

Historic icons like Da Vinci, Benjamin Franklin, and Abraham Lincoln each left their imprint on society because of their change leadership. Roosevelt, Martin Luther King, Elvis, and Steve Jobs helped change generations of people throughout the world. Facebook founder Mark Zuckerberg, and Google founders Larry Page and Sergey Brin represent a new generation of change leaders for the twenty-first century. The traits or characteristics of these change leaders are remarkably similar, supporting the notion that change leadership is a human skill or form of intellect that transcends generations. Obviously, the intellect can be present in any societal or cultural mix.

Each of these change leaders confirms the melding of various intelligences and the uniqueness of change leadership intelligence (CLQ). These change leaders suggest an unconventional way of thinking that may fall outside the norm of society. Arguably, change leaders are visionaries who do not conform to societal standards; instead they create new standards for society that are often beyond the scope of everyday thinking.

Supporting Models

Exploring change models from the literature may help guide a definition of change leadership intelligence (CLQ). The first-to-change mover advantage triangle (FCMA) by Rideout (2012) provides a systems perspective for understanding the change management process (see Appendix B). The model resulted from research questions during a Delphi study involving leaders from the U.S. metal building industry. Using study data to support the underlying research questions, Rideout identified specific strategies to manage the change process in the organization, and translated this into the FCMA.

The FCMA is a four-step process leaders may use to guide change management. According to Rideout (2012), leaders should: 1) develop strategies to identify and forecast change, 2) differentiate between internal and external change forces, 3) develop a response to the change forces, and 4) use the change forces to create a competitive advantage. These steps suggest organizations may gain a distinct advantage based on the leader's ability to identify and manage change in advance of competitors.

Kotter (1996) and Bishop (2001) offered similar change process models, and support FCMA assertions. Kotter identified eight steps for managing change including creating urgency, developing a coalition in the organization to gain support, and using successes to implement and promote future change. Bishop outlined a change process condensed in three stages 1) assessment, 2) creating the plan, and 3) gauging readiness for change. The FCMA expands on the Kotter, and Bishop models by stressing the influence of forces in the internal and external environment, and how these forces precipitate or create the need to change. This philosophy coincides with the Senge (2006) argument that without systems' thinking organizational leadership may not be able to

20

account for the forces that influence and possibly hinder making future visions a reality.

Defining, Assessing, and Developing CLQ

Positing a working definition of change leadership intelligence (CLQ) requires melding theory and real-world application. Using the literature review, and other supporting text, including examples of change leaders in society, a formal definition may be constructed. CLQ may be described as an individual's ability to embrace, identify, manage, and promote change to create a leadership position personally and professionally.

The CLQ Wheel (see Appendix C) provides visualization, including the cognitive CLQ developmental process. The Wheel shows the influence of the intelligences that support CLQ during each process. For instance, embracing change links to the self, requiring the learner to develop his or her emotional intelligence. The shape of the Wheel (circular) provides a systems perspective suggesting the integrated nature when developing and learning to use CLQ, and that learning is continuous. Lastly, the Wheel suggests an end result when developing heightened CLQ, becoming a change rebel. A rebel may be described as someone who defies or resists conforming to societal norms (Anonymous, 1996). A person with heightened CLQ or a change rebel does not accept the norm, but instead embraces, identifies, manages, and promotes change or being different. Becoming a change rebel may be the new norm for the twenty-first century.

Change leadership intelligence (CLQ) is a byproduct of cultural, emotional, logical and mathematical, practical, and social intelligences. Synergizing the strengths of these intelligences with systems theory creates the foundation for CLQ, a unique twenty-first century intelligence, suggesting people may become change leaders, personally and professionally, by developing and learning to use a range of melded intelligences. The specific strengths CLQ draws from each intelligence and systems theory include:

- Cultural–ability to accept new environments;
- Emotional–comfort with 'self' to accept change;
- Logical and Mathematical–ability to think deductively and draw links and conclusions;
- Practical–common sense aspect of change;
- Social–heightened awareness of external environment; and

- Systems Theory–appreciation for integrated nature of the world.

The relationship of each intelligence and systems theory to CLQ may be expressed by C+E+LM+P+S+ST = CLQ

Creating an assessment tool to measure change leadership intelligence (CLQ) requires a broad instrument measuring multiple areas. These areas include a) embracing, b) identifying, c) managing, and d) promoting change. The CLQ Wheel (see Appendix C) suggests change leadership intelligence is a cognitive process. Each process builds on the other as the individual develops his or her skills. See Appendix D for a potential assessment tool outline.

Conclusions

Benjamin Franklin once said there are two certainties in life, death and taxes. Many would agree that change is a third certainty. We all encounter it regularly, some heeding it more often than others. Biologically change must be occurring constantly. We all have to admit this and learn to savor it. That's not exactly a popular idea among those who want to "turn back the clock" as the ads say. The answer is learning how to overcome the challenges associated with change. The key lies somewhere in the chasm of willingness to learn a new way of thinking, to discover a higher understanding of how change works. Perhaps more important, learning how to transform change into a positive event may redefine the course of what truly is a competitive advantage. CLQ provides a potential pathway for achieving this.

References

Albrecht, K. (2006). *Social intelligence: The new science of success.* San Francisco: Jossey-Bass.

Albrecht, K. (2007). *Practical intelligence: The art and science of common sense.* New York, NY: Jossey-Bass.

Anonymous. (1996). *Webster's II new riverside dictionary.* Boston, MA: Houghton Mifflin Company.

Arora, N. (2003). *Theory zyx of successful change management: A definitive practical guide to reach the next level.* L.A. Press.

Bellanca, J., Chapman, C., & Swartz, E. (1997). *Multiple assessments for multiple intelligences* (3rd ed.). Arlington Heights, IL: Skylight Training and Publishing, Inc.

Bennis, W., & Goldsmith, J. (1997). *Learning to lead: A workbook on becoming a leader.* Reading, MA: Perseus Books.

Bishop, C. H. (2001). *Making change happen one person at a time.* New York, NY: AMACOM.

Boulding, K. E. (1956). General systems theory -- The skeleton of science. *Management Science, 2*(3), 197-208.

Charan, R. (2009). *Leadership in the era of economic uncertainty.* New York: McGraw-Hill.

Drucker, P. F. (1999). *Management challenges for the 21st century.* New York, NY: Harper Business.

Earley, P. C., & Mosakowski, E. (2004). Cultural intelligence. *Harvard Business Review, 82*(10), 139.

Facione, P. A. (2011). Critical thinking: What it is and why it counts. *Insight Assessment.*

Fiedler, F. E. (1981). Leadership effectiveness: Emergent leadership what makes the leader effective? Situational factors determining the role of intelligence and experience in leadership performance. *The American Behavioral Scientist (pre-1986), 24*(5), 619.

Gardner, H. (1983). *Frames of mind: The theory of multiple intelligences.* New York, NY: Basic Books.

Gardner, H. (1999). *Intelligence reframed: Multiple intelligences for the 21st century.* New York, NY: Basic Books.

Goleman, D. (1995). *Emotional intelligence: Why it can matter more than IQ.* New York, NY: Bantam Books.

Goleman, D. (1998). What makes a leader? *Harvard Business Review, 76*(6), 93-102.

Hamel, G., & Prahalad, C. K. (1994). *Competing for the future.* Boston, MA: Harvard Business School Press.

Hoffer, E. (1952). *The ordeal of change.* New York, NY: Harper & Row.

Johnson, R. A., Kast, F. E., & Rosenzweig, J. E. (1964). Systems theory and management. *Management Science, 10*(2), 367-384.

Kanter, R. M. (1983). *The change masters.* New York, NY: Simon & Schuster.

Kotter, J. P. (1996). *Leading change.* Boston, MA: Harvard Business School Press.

Landale, A. (2004). Being a leader of change. *The British Journal of Administrative Management,* 18.

Laszlo, E. (1996). *The systems view of the world: A holistic vision for our time.* Cresskill, NJ: Hampton Press.

Mann, J. (2010). Futurists vs. planners: Given the rapid speed of business today, forward-thinking companies should consider futurology to stay ahead of change. (Future View). *The Futurist, 36*, 68.

McLean, J. (2007). Prepare for the future. It's happening fast! *The British Journal of Administrative Management*, 17.

Mockler, R. J. (1968). The systems approach to business organization and decision making. *California Management Review, 11*(2), 53-58.

Peters, R. (1987). *Practical intelligence: Working smarter in business and the professions*. New York NY: Harper & Row Publishers.

Philley, J. (2005). Critical thinking concepts. *Professional Safety, 50*(3), 26-26-32.

Rideout, G. W. (2012). *Change leadership: A U.S. metal building industry perspective*. Charleston, SC: Evolution Strategists Press.

Salovey, P., & Mayer, J. D. (1990). Emotional intelligence. *Imagination, Cognition, and Personality*, 9, 185-211. Retrieved from http://www.unh.edu/emotional_intelligence/EI%20Assets /Reprints...EI%20Proper/EI1990%20Emotional%20Intelligen ce.pdf

Senge, P. M. (2006). *The fifth discipline: The art and practice of a learning organization*. New York, NY: DOUBLEDAY.

Sternberg, R. J., Forsythe, G. B., Hedlund, J., Horvath, J. A., Wagner, R. K., Williams, W. M., et al. (2000). *Practical intelligence in everyday life*. New York, NY: Cambridge University Press.

Sternberg, R. J., Kaufman, J. C., & Grigorenko, E. L. (2008). *Applied intelligence*. New York, NY: Cambridge University Press.

Toffler, A. (1970). *Future shock*. New York, NY: Bantam Books.

Triandis, H. C. (2006). Cultural intelligence in organizations. *Group & Organization Management, 31*(1), 20. doi: 10.1177/1059601105275253

Tuominen, K. (2000). *Managing change: Practical strategies for competitive advantage*. Milwaukee, WI: ASQ.

Ulrich, D. (1996). Credibility x capability. In F. Hesselbein, M. Goldsmith & R. Beckhard (Eds.), *The leader of the future*. San Francisco, CA: Jossey-Bass.

Von Bertalanffy, L. (1969). *General system theory: Foundations, development, applications*. New York, NY: George Braziller.

Zori, S., & Morrison, B. (2009). Critical thinking in nurse managers. *Nursing Economics, 27*(2), 75-75-79, and 98.

Appendix A

Suggested Readings

Adcroft, A., Willis, R., & Hurst, J. (2008). A new model for managing change: The holistic view. *The Journal of Business Strategy, 29*(1), 40. doi: 10.1108/02756660810845697

Alas, R., & Sun, W. (2007). Organizational changes in Chinese companies: A resource-based view. *Chinese Management Studies, 1*(4), 225.

Andrews, J., Cameron, H., & Harris, M. (2008). All change? Managers' experience of organizational change in theory and practice. *Journal of Organizational Change Management, 21*(3), 300.

Anonymous. (2003). Change management models-making the right decisions. *Futurics, 27*(1/2), 85-85.

Axelrod, R. H., Axelrod, E., Jacobs, R. W., & Beedon, J. (2006). Beat the odds and succeed in organizational change. *Consulting to Management, 17*(2), 6.

Beitler, M. A. (2006). *Strategic organizational change: A practitioner's guide for managers and consultants* (2nd ed.). Greensboro, NC: Practitioner Press International.

Bennis, W. G. (1992). Managing the dream: Leadership in the 21st century. *Management Decision, 30*(6), 166.

Bititci, U. S. (2007). An executive's guide to business transformation. *Business Strategy Series, 8*(3), 203.

Bjelland, O. M., & Wood, R. C. (2008). Five ways to transform a business. *Strategy & Leadership, 36*(3), 4. doi: 10.1108/10878570810870730

Boyatzis, R. E., & Akrivou, K. (2006). The ideal self as the driver of intentional change. *The Journal of Management Development, 25*(7), 624.

Boyatzis, R., & McKee, A. (2006). Intentional change. *Journal of Organizational Excellence.* doi: 10.1002/joe.20100

Burnes, B. (2005). Complexity theories and organizational change. *International Journal of Management Reviews, 7*(2), 73-90. doi: 10.1111/j.1468-2370.2005.00107.x

Carter, E. (2008). Successful change requires more than change management. *The Journal for Quality and Participation, 31*(1), 20.

Cheng, L. R. L. (2007). Cultural intelligence (CQ): A quest for cultural competence. *Communication Disorders Quarterly, 29*(1), 36. doi: 10.1177/1525740108314860

Chrusciel, D. (2006). Considerations of emotional intelligence (EI) in dealing with change decision management. *Management Decision, 44*(5), 644-657. doi: 10.1108/00251740610668897

Colletti, J. A., & Chonko, L. B. (1997). Change management initiatives: Moving sales organizations from obsolescence to high performance. *The Journal of Personal Selling & Sales Management, 17*(2), 1.

de Jager, P. (2001). Resistance to change: A new view of an old problem. *The Futurist, 35*(3), 24-27.

Denning, S. (2011). Reinventing management: The practices that enable continuous innovation. *Strategy & Leadership, 39*(3), 16-24. doi: 10.1108/10878571111128775

Eales-White, R. (2005). Harnessing the power of paradigms. *Industrial and Commercial Training, 37*(6/7), 291.

Erwin, D., & Garman, A. (2010). Resistance to organizational change: Linking research and practice. *Leadership & Organization Development Journal, 31*(1), 39-56. doi: 10.1108/01437731011010371

Ferres, N., & Connell, J. (2004). Emotional intelligence in leaders: An antidote for cynicism towards change? *Strategic Change, 13*(2), 61. doi: 10.1002/jsc.665

Folaron, J. (2005). The human side of change leadership. *Quality Progress, 38*(4), 39-43.

Fulmer, R. M. (1994). A model for changing the way organizations learn. *Strategy & Leadership, 22*(3), 20-20.

Galán, J., Monje, J., & Zúñiga-Vicente, J. (2009). Implementing change in smaller firms. *Research Technology Management, 52*(1), 59.

Harper, S. C., & Glew, D. J. (2008). Becoming an ever-evolving enterprise. *Industrial Management, 50*(3), 22.

Holland, W. E. (2000). *Change is the rule: Practical actions for change on time, on target, on budget.* Chicago: Dearborn

Joroff, M. L., Porter, W. L., Feinberg, B., & Kukla, C. (2003). The agile workplace. *Journal of Corporate Real Estate, 5*(4), 293.

Knippen, J. T., & Green, T. B. (1997). How to respond to change. *Journal of Workplace Learning, 9*(1), 17-17-19.

Kyriacou, D. N. (2004). Evidence-based medical decision making: Deductive versus inductive logical thinking. *Academic Emergency Medicine, 11*(6), 670-670-671.

Lazear, D. (1994). *Multiple intelligence approaches to assessment: Solving the assessment conundrum.* Tucson, AZ: Zephyr Press.

Léon de, C., & Vermaak, H. (2004). Change paradigms: An overview. *Organization Development Journal, 22*(4), 9.

Lewis, L. K., Schmisseur, A. M., Stephens, K. K., & Weir, K. E. (2006). Advice on communicating during organizational change. *Journal of Business Communication, 43*(2), 113-137.

Maccoby, M. (2010). Learn change leadership from two great teachers. *Research Technology Management, 53*(2), 68.

Marine, A., & Riley, P. (1995). Creating a culture of change. *Hospital materiel management quarterly, 16*(4), 30.

Robertson, S. (2007). Got EQ? Increasing cultural and clinical competence through emotional intelligence. *Communication Disorders Quarterly, 29*(1), 14. doi: 10.1177/1525740108314864

Thomas, D. C. (2006). Domain and development of cultural intelligence: The importance of mindfulness. *Group & Organization Management, 31*(1), 78. doi: 10.1177/1059601105275266

Watson, G. (1971). Resistance to change. *The American Behavioral Scientist (pre-1986), 14*(5), 745-745.

Wieand, P., Birchfield, J., & Johnson, M., III. (2008). The new leadership challenge: Removing the emotional barriers to sustainable performance in a flat world. *Ivey Business Journal Online*.

Yeo, R. (2002). From individual to team learning: Practical perspectives on the learning organisation. *Team Performance Management, 8*(7/8), 157-170.

Yuthas, K., Dillard, J. F., & Rogers, R. K. (2004). Beyond agency and structure: Triple-Loop learning. *Journal of Business Ethics, 51*(2), 229-243.

Zand, D. E., & Sorensen, R. E. (1975). Theory of change and the effective use of management science. *Administrative Science Quarterly, 20*(4), 532-545.

Zieglar, J. G. (2003). Toward a synthesis of decision-making and change management. *Futurics, 27*(1/2), 77-77.

Zimmerman, J. (2004). Leading organizational change is like climbing a mountain. *The Educational Forum, 68*(3).

Zurewich, J. A. (2008). A general theory of change. *Humanomics, 24*(4), 263.

Appendix B

The FCMA Triangle

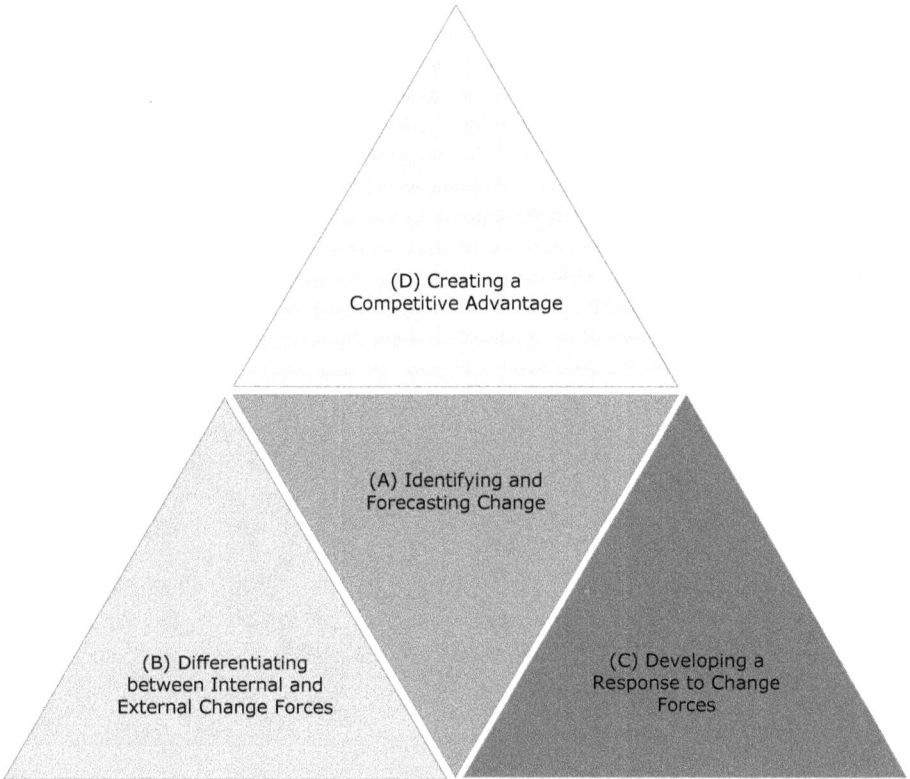

Appendix C

The CLQ Wheel

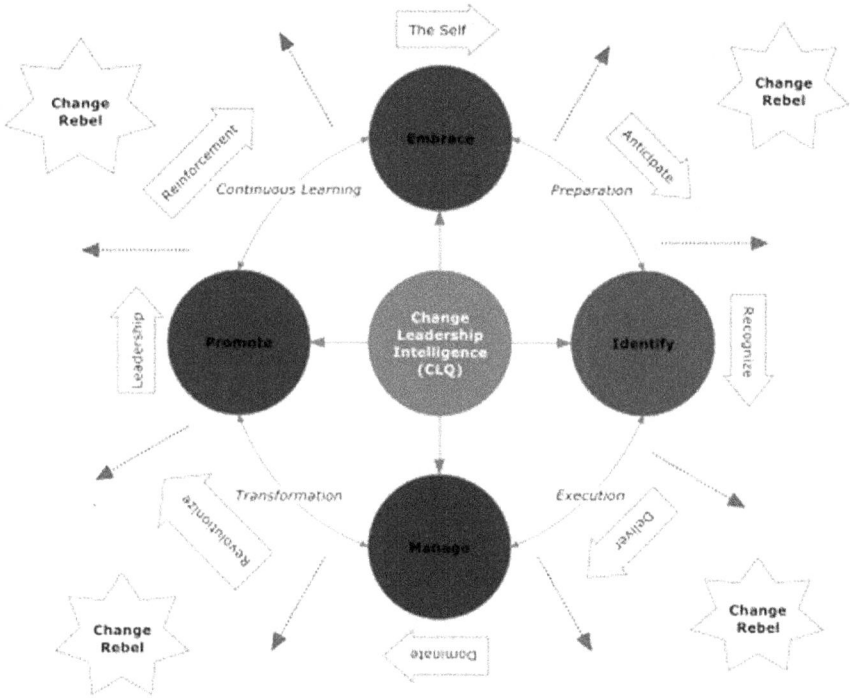

Appendix D

CLQ Assessment Outline

Four-part cognitive-based assessment of change leadership intelligence (CLQ):

I.   Embrace Change (the ability to accept change) answers the questions:
   a.   Who are you?
   b.   Do you know your real self?
   c.   How do you feel in your skin?
   d.   Do you have the right attitude?
   e.   Do you have the right mindset?
   f.   Are you afraid of the unknown?
   g.   Are you well read?
   h.   Are you prepared to anticipate change comfortably?

II.   Identify Change (the ability to distinguish change in environment) answers the questions:
   a.   Can you distinguish between short and long-term change?
   b.   Can you separate whims from real change forces?
   c.   Can you bridge the gap between recognizing change and creating a viable plan to execute?
   d.   Can you create a future vision state?
   e.   Are you an inductive or deductive thinker?
   f.   Are you prepared to create and deliver the change you see in the environment?

III.   Manage Change (the ability to take change from a vision state to reality and persevere to fruition) answers the questions:
   a.   Can you manage the stress, the grind, and the frustration?
   b.   Are you prepared to transform the change initiative (what you have accomplished) into a leadership position?
   c.   Are you ready to overcome the competition?
   d.   Do you have the tenacity?

IV.   Promote (ability to use change to create a leadership position personally and professionally) answers the questions:
   a.   Do you know how to become a continuous learner?
   b.   Are you ready to become a creator instead of a follower?
   c.   Do you want your competitors to envy and emulate you?

About the Author

George W. Rideout, D.B.A., is a principal for Evolution Strategists LLC and executive director of the Change Leadership Intelligence (CLQ) Institute. Dr. Rideout holds an MBA and numerous professional certifications, including the certified six sigma black belt (CSSBB), and the FCIB international certified credit executive (ICCE). He is a published author and frequent speaker, with more than 16 years' experience in sales and management. His research interests include change leadership, decision-making, leadership studies, multiple intelligences, and systems theories.

www.ingramcontent.com/pod-product-compliance
Lightning Source LLC
Chambersburg PA
CBHW060625030426
42337CB00018B/3199